LITURGY AND CONTEMPLATION

Jacques and Raïssa Maritain

LITURGY and

CONTEMPLATION

translated from the French by Joseph W. Evans

P. J. KENEDY & SONS · NEW YORK

Nihil obstat: MYLES M. BOURKE, S.T.D.
        Censor Librorum

Imprimatur: ✠ FRANCIS CARDINAL SPELLMAN
        Archbishop of New York

New York
February 10, 1960

The nihil obstat and imprimatur are official declarations that a book or pamphlet is free of doctrinal or moral error. No implication is contained therein that those who have granted the nihil obstat and imprimatur agree with the contents, opinions or statements expressed.

CONTENTS

ACKNOWLEDGMENT

is made to *Spiritual Life,* the
quarterly review in which this
work substantially appeared

PART ONE
ON LITURGY

✝ ·

CHAPTER I

Liturgy and the interior life

The general theme of this study is that there is an intimate relationship between liturgy and contemplation, and that it would be as absurd to wish to sacrifice contemplation to liturgy as to wish to sacrifice liturgy to contemplation. As Pope Pius XII put it, "no conflict exists . . . between the ascetical life and devotion to the Liturgy." [1] Furthermore, the liturgy itself asks that the soul tend to contemplation; and participation in the liturgical life, if it is understood and practiced in its true spirit, is an outstanding preparation for union with God by contemplation of love.

Before beginning we wish to pay tribute to the memory of Dom Virgil Michel, whose friendship was dear to us, and who was the great pioneer

[1] Encyclical *Mediator Dei* (November 20, 1947), p. 18. Here and elsewhere we refer to the Vatican Library translation, *The Sacred Liturgy*, printed by the National Catholic Welfare Conference, Washington, D. C.

of the liturgical movement in America. This movement, which is linked in this country to an especially generous apostolate, is now undergoing, as
was clearly evident at the 19th North American
Liturgical Week held in Cincinnati in August of
1958, a considerable expansion.[2] It is with the
hope of contributing our modest share to this
movement that we shall discuss certain opinions
which have taken, here and there in Europe, a
systematic form,[3] and the practical influence of
which, we are told, is not without making itself
felt here—opinions which can only hurt the liturgical movement, because they go counter to the
spirit of the liturgy.

*

The liturgy is the public worship of the Church,
the public worship rendered to God by the Mystical Body of Christ. "The sacred Liturgy is the public worship which our Redeemer as Head of the
Church renders to the Father as well as the worship which the community of the faithful renders
to its Founder, and through Him to the Heavenly

[2] On the liturgical movement in America, see the remarkable
study published by *Jubilee,* August, 1958.
[3] Need we recall the controversies raised by Dom Festugière
in 1913–1914?

Father. It is, in short, the worship rendered by the Mystical Body of Christ in the entirety of its Head and members." [4]

This public worship has for its center the sacrifice of the Mass. It is, of course, and of necessity, "exterior" [5] and "social." [6] The singing, the psalms, the rites, the continuous teaching drawn from Holy Scripture and the Fathers, the great vocal prayer of the Church are as a living garland around the Holy Sacrifice publicly offered and the sacraments visibly distributed.

But this public worship is also, and must be, principally interior. Otherwise it would become empty formalism. [7] This is one of the points that the encyclical *Mediator Dei* stresses most forcefully and to which it returns most often. "The chief element of divine worship must be interior. For we must always live in Christ and give ourselves to Him completely, so that in Him, with Him and through Him the heavenly Father may be duly glorified." [8] Liturgical worship requires of

---

[4] *Mediator Dei*, p. 10.

[5] *Ibid.*, pp. 11–12.

[6] *Ibid.*, p. 12.

[7] "The sacred Liturgy requires (us) . . . 'to give inferior effect to our outward observance' (*Missale Rom.*, Secreta Feriae V post Dom. II Quadrag.). Otherwise religion clearly amounts to mere formalism, without meaning and without content." *Ibid.*, p. 12.

[8] *Ibid.*, p. 12.

those who participate in it "meditation on the supernatural realities" [9] and "ascetic effort prompt-
ing them to purify their hearts" [10]; it is above all by
an act hidden in the innermost depths of themselves, invisible to men and not heard by them, it
is above all by interior fervor of soul and by unit-
ing their hearts with the intentions of the celebrant
and with those of the Eternal Priest, that the faithful offer with Him the sacrifice and offer themselves with Him. [11]

We are here, we believe, in the presence of a central truth. What is principal in the New Law, Saint
Thomas Aquinas teaches, is the grace of the Holy
Spirit operating in hearts.[12] It is accordingly to internal and invisible reality that major importance
has henceforth passed. This law of interiorization,
which is characteristic of the New Testament,
does not apply only to moral life, where henceforth it is interior movements and their purity
which count first. It applies also to worship itself.
The worship rendered to God by the Church is
necessarily an exterior worship, but it is a worship
in spirit and in truth, in which what matters above

[9] *Ibid.*, p. 15.
[10] *Ibid.*, p. 17.
[11] Cf. *ibid.*, pp. 36–9.
[12] *Sum. theol.*, I–II, 107, 1, ad 2 and ad 3.

all is the interior movement of souls and the divine grace operating in them. Consequently, Catholic liturgy requires—in order that the public worship rendered to God be authentic and real, and really *dignum et justum*—that the theological virtues be at work in those who participate in it; Catholic liturgy lives on faith, hope and charity. "God is to be worshipped," Saint Augustine says, "by faith, hope and charity." [13]

What is this to say, if not that Catholic liturgy asks that those who participate in it tend to the perfection of charity—"it should be clear to all," Pius XII says, "that God cannot be honored worthily unless the mind and heart turn to Him in quest of the perfect life" [14]—and that it asks at the same stroke·that they cultivate interior recollection and aspire to union with God, in other words, that they tend, even if from afar, to something which is beyond simple participation in liturgical worship, and which is accomplished in the secret of hearts?

[13] *Enchiridion,* cap. 3. Cited by the encyclical *Mediator Dei,* p. 21. Saint Thomas says: "The theological virtues, faith, hope and charity, whose act has for its object God Himself, give rise to and govern the act of religion, which has for its object certain things-to-be-done directed towards God." *Sum. theol.,* II–II, 81, 5, ad 1.

[14] *Mediator Dei,* p. 13.

Two crucial truths—to which we shall give more attention in the second part of this study —are at stake here. On the one hand, all are held by the divine precept to tend to the perfection of charity, each one according to his condition and his possibilities. And it is clear that if this precept is violated, in other words, (if charity is not in the soul, there is no worship rendered to God in spirit and in truth.)

On the other hand, the call of all to the perfection of charity has for corollary the call of all— call proximate or remote—to enter into the ways of the spirit and to participate, to one degree or another, in that loving attention to God and that dialogue of love with God which, susceptible of the most diverse modes, and compatible with the active life as with the contemplative life, have their highest point in the contemplation of the saints.

Let us not be misunderstood here. We do not claim that those who participate in the liturgical life of the Church should all be in some degree contemplatives and have passed under the regime of the gifts of the Holy Spirit. On the contrary, it is the whole mass of the Christian people—the weak, the negligent, the ignorant and the reluctant in the spiritual life, as well as those who are already the true disciples of Christ—that the great sacred movement of the liturgy draws along, stimulates and instructs. But to what does it draw them, what does it teach them, if not to stammer divine things and to aspire, even if from very far, to some beginning at least of contemplation and of union with God? What we are saying is that it is normal that those who participate in the liturgical life *tend* to enter to some degree into the contemplation of the saints, and to practice accordingly mental prayer under some form and to some degree. "The author of that golden book *The Imitation of Christ* certainly speaks in accordance with the letter and the spirit of the Liturgy, when he gives the following advice to the person who approaches the altar: 'Remain on in secret and take delight in your God; for He is yours Whom the whole world cannot take away from you' (Lib. IV, cap. 12)." [15]

Not to speak of the great Saint Gertrude, let us invoke in confirmation of this truth a very signifi-

---

[15] *Ibid.,* p. 46. "All these things [in the sacred Liturgy]"—Pius XII also teaches, recalling the Council of Trent—"*aim* at 'enhancing the majesty of this great Sacrifice, and raising the minds of the faithful by means of these visible signs of religion and piety, *to the contemplation of the sublime truths contained in this Sacrifice.*' " *Ibid.,* pp. 37–8 (italics ours).

cant modern witness: one of the most beautiful books on mental prayer and contemplation that has been written by an author whose whole life was consecrated to the *opus Dei*—Madame Cécile Bruyère, Abbess of Sainte-Cécile de Solesmes.[16]

[16] Madame Cécile Bruyère, Abbess of Sainte-Cécile, *La Vie spirituelle et l'Oraison* (the most recent edition was published in Tours by Maison Mame in 1949–1950).

CHAPTER II

Liturgy and the Church's contemplation

The liturgical cycle manifests in sacred signs the states of Christ and the participation of the Mystical Body in "the mysteries of His humiliation, of His redemption and triumph." [17] "Hence the Liturgical Year devotedly fostered and accompanied by the Church, is not a cold and lifeless representation of the events of the past. . . . It is rather Christ Himself Who is ever living in His Church. Here He continues that journey of immense mercy which He lovingly began in His mortal life. . . ." [18]

It is clear, however, that the states of Christ such as they were lived in the intimacy of His soul are something greater than the signs of the sacred cycle which manifest them.

Likewise, as concerns the Church or the Mysti-

[17] *Mediator Dei,* p. 53.
[18] *Ibid.,* p. 57.

cal Body, something is greater—not certainly
than the Holy Sacrifice (about which we shall
speak later on)—but greater than the very sub-
limity of the lessons, of the prayers and the singing, of the sacred rites and symbols through which
the cycle of the seasons and the feasts unfolds, and
which manifest the participation of the Church in
the states of the Lord; this something greater is
this very participation itself, in so far as it is lived
in the intimacy of the soul by the Church in her
saints, and, to some degree, in the immense multitude of her members in the state of grace. In other
words, it is the suffering and the love through
which the Church applies all along the course of
time the merits and the blood of Christ; and it is
the contemplation of the Church, that contemplation which enables it to experience in some way
the mysteries of God the Savior, and which takes
place, through the grace of the Holy Spirit who is
the soul of the Church, in human persons joined
together as one in its communion.

This contemplation of the Church, in which the
grace of the theological virtues and of the gifts of
the Holy Spirit expands in the invisible recesses of
hearts, is clearly superior to the great liturgical
voice which manifests it; *quantum potes, tantum*

aude: thanksgiving, praise, petition, the liturgical service never succeeds—no matter how pure its élan may be, no matter how ardent its rapture— in manifesting this contemplation of the Mystical Body in an entirely adequate manner, for in itself it is ineffable. It is to it that the liturgy wishes to lead souls, and it is from it that the liturgy super-abounds.

Now, what is true of the Mystical Body is clearly true, proportionately, of the individuals who are its members. In what concerns individual souls, contemplation, to the extent that they attain to it, is superior to the acts through which they take part in the divine service.

Some err because, comparing the contemplation of one soul in particular with the liturgy of the whole Church, they say that contemplation is only a singular act of an individual, whereas the liturgical life is the common act of the Mystical Body itself. In reality, it is the participation *of such or such a one in particular* in the liturgical life, that is to be compared with the contemplation of *such or such a one in particular*.

One also errs when one claims that in contemplation the person acts as a particular whole or particular individual, whereas in participation in

the liturgical life he acts as a part and member of
that Whole which is the Church or the Mystical
Body itself. In reality, just as for an individual
soul, to sing the Divine Office is to participate in
the liturgical life of the Church, so also for an individual soul to contemplate God lovingly is to
participate in the contemplation of the Church:
because it is the property of the Mystical Body,
supernatural society living by the grace of Christ
and of the Holy Spirit, to embrace in the whole
that it constitutes and in its communion all that
there is of the most intimate and the most personal
in the most highly personal activity of the particular persons who are its members.

One too often overlooks this truth, which has
to do essentially with the very difference between
the supernatural society which is the Church and
every other society or community. Never is a man
more a member, and more perfectly a member, of
the Church than when, *clauso ostio* and alone with
Him Whom he loves, he is united to God in an
ineffable union of person to person, and enters
into the depths of God. The one who, like Saint
Anthony in the desert or Saint John of the Cross
in his dungeon, is united to God by infused prayer,
participates more in the life of the Mystical Body

than those who by their words and their gestures —and with piety doubtless, but supposing they have not crossed the threshold of infused contemplation—follow the rubrics of the liturgy with the greatest exactitude. For it is in what there is of the most intimate and the most profound in the Church that such a one thus participates: in his love for God and for men there courses invisibly something of the love which God infuses into the entire Church, and it is from the divine sources themselves of the life of the Church coursing through his heart and causing him to act as part of it, in other words, it is from the grace of Christ and the inspiration of the Holy Spirit that the contemplative union proceeds in him. In the midst of what is the more personal thing in the world he is a member of the Church more than ever and by highest right.

CHAPTER III

The virtue of religion and the theological virtues

To say that simple participation in the liturgical worship, no matter how attentive and exact one supposes it, carries the spiritual life to a more elevated degree than infused contemplation and consequently dispenses from all aspiration and preparation for it, would be to reverse the order of things, and to have a moral virtue—the virtue of religion—take precedence over the theological virtues and the gifts of the Holy Spirit.

On the one hand, indeed, infused contemplation depends essentially on the theological virtues and the gifts of the Holy Spirit, and is their common operation itself, through which the soul, carried to a superhuman mode of acting, is joined to God and enters into the depths of God.

On the other hand, worship and the liturgy depend essentially on the virtue of religion; and the virtue of religion, as Saint Thomas teaches, hav-

ing for its object *not directly God Himself* but
*something to be done, certain acts to be accom-
plished* with respect to God and to honor God, is
not a theological virtue; it is a moral virtue,[19] however eminent it may be,[20] and it therefore remains
subordinate to the theological virtues [21] and to the
gifts of the Holy Spirit.[22]

Thus liturgical worship is in itself an end of
very great dignity; and yet there is a higher end—
an end for which, and the longing for which, it
must normally dispose souls. As we noted above,[23]
liturgical worship implies the exercise of the theological virtues—it lives on faith, hope and charity,
which give rise to and govern the acts of religion.
But of itself it is a work—the noblest, most resplendent and holiest work—of the moral virtue
which is the virtue of religion. And it asks of those
who take part in it that they ascend, to the extent
that they are able, towards that summit where the
theological virtues produce, under the inspiration
of the Holy Spirit, an interior act which surpasses

[19] *Sum. theol.*, II–II, 81, 5.
[20] For Saint Thomas it is the most excellent of the moral virtues. *Ibid.*, a. 6.
[21] *Sum. theol.*, II–II, 81, 5. Cf. *ibid.*, 82, 2, ad 1: "Charity is the principle of religion."
[22] Like the theological virtues, *the gifts are of higher value than the moral virtues,* II–II, 81, 2, ad 1.
[23] See above, note 13.

every operation of the human being externally
manifested, in particular those operations which
express by voice and gesture our union with the
community of the faithful.

But is there not in Catholic worship something
which surpasses the human order altogether? Yes,
certainly. Not only indeed is it essential to Christian worship, to worship in spirit and in truth, to
put into play the three theological virtues; but
God Himself intervenes in the worship which is
rendered to Him, God Himself is present at the
center of the liturgy. The center of the liturgy is
Holy Mass, the sacrifice of the Cross perpetuated
on the altar, the unbloody immolation in which,
through the ministry of the earthly priest, the Eternal Priest offers Himself as a victim to His Father;
the center of the liturgy is an act of an infinite and
infinitely transcendent value, an act properly divine, without common measure with the highest
works of grace in the human soul: because it is an
act of God (using the instrumentality of the
priest), not an act of man.

We must conclude from this, on the one hand,
that the more elevated a soul is in infused contemplation and the ways of the spirit, the more
profound will be its devotion to the Mass and the

more ardent its desire to unite itself to it; and, on the other hand, that to assist at Mass with dispositions which are in some way proportioned to the act which is accomplished on the altar, the highest contemplation would be required—though no contemplation, no matter how high it might be, will ever be truly proportioned to the divine mystery of the altar, which asks of love and the living faith of the soul, and of its purifications, ever and ever more.

Hence it is that what the liturgy asks of the soul, and that to which it stirs it, the liturgy itself alone does not suffice to give to the soul. Personal ascetical effort, personal practice of mental prayer, personal aspiration to union with God, and personal docility to the gifts of the Holy Spirit are necessary.

It would thus be a great error to conclude from the truths we have just recalled, that in what concerns the human beings that we are, and the acts which emanate from us, assistance at the divine act of the Mass makes superfluous these different aspects of personal effort towards the intimate perfection of the soul.[24]

[24] ". . . Christ after redeeming the world at the lavish cost of His own Blood, still must come into complete possession of

It would likewise be a great error to conclude that simple participation in the liturgy would establish our spiritual life at a more elevated degree than the one to which it is drawn by union with God in contemplation.

---

the souls of men. Wherefore, that the redemption and salvation of each person and of future generations unto the end of time may be effectively accomplished, and be acceptable to God, it is necessary that men should individually come into vital contact with the Sacrifice of the Cross, so that the merits which flow from it should be imparted to them. In a certain sense it can be said that on Calvary Christ built a font of purification and salvation, which He filled with the Blood He shed; but if men do not bathe in it and there wash away the stains of their iniquities, they can never be purified and saved." *Mediator Dei,* p. 30.

PART TWO

ON CONTEMPLATION

CHAPTER I

Infused contemplation

But what is contemplation in itself? Contemplation is a silent prayer which takes place in recollection in the secret of the heart, and is directly ordered to union with God.

It is an ascent of the soul towards God, or rather an attraction of the soul towards Him, for the sake of Him.

When a soul becomes free enough to speak of itself, when God wills it, it describes its state of mental prayer, to the extent that this is possible. And it is thus that there reaches us the account of admirable experiences which awakens in hearts the desire for this recollection in God, and for the seeking of spiritual perfection—for love of Him.

It is for this that among a great many other great saints and souls of grace, a Saint Teresa, for example, and a Saint John of the Cross, Doctor of the Church, received the gift of describing in their words the experience and science of the mystical life and of mental prayer. Saint John of the Cross spoke of it in prose, and in poems of a unique beauty. And very often saintly souls who have had the experience of spiritual things have also received the graceful gift of speaking of it in a beautiful, persuasive and luminous way.

In this wholly interior light live Faith, Hope, Charity. And by the gifts of the Holy Spirit "the soul is directed and moved immediately by divine inspiration." [1]

> *Without light or guide, save that*
> *which burned in my heart,* [2]

says Saint John of the Cross, as he passes through the dark night which he knew so profoundly. But it is the fire of the Holy Spirit which accounts for the ardor of this light.

According to the common teaching of the theologians, it is at once on the theological virtues, supernatural in their essence, and on the gifts of the Holy Spirit, "doubly supernatural—supernatural not only in their essence, like the theological

[1] Garrigou-Lagrange, *Perfection chrétienne et Contemplation* (Paris: Desclée & Cie), 5ᵉ éd., t. I, p. 34.
[2] *Dark Night of the Soul*, Stanza 3 (translation of E. Allison Peers).

virtues, but in their mode of action," [3] that infused contemplation and the mystical life depend.

Let us recall the definition—a very general one —that Father Lallemant, the great spiritual writer of the 17th century, gives of contemplation: "Contemplation is a viewing of God or of divine things, simple, free, penetrating, which proceeds from love and tends toward love. . . . It is the use of the purest and most perfect charity. Love is its source, its exercise and its end." [4]

We are speaking here, as is Father Lallemant, of infused contemplation, and with all the more reason since it is infused contemplation which is being disregarded today by certain minds who would like to reduce the whole spiritual life to liturgical piety; and we are speaking of infused contemplation in abstraction from the variety presented by the states of mental prayer and the diverse degrees of union.

The thesis that all souls are called, not doubtless in a proximate manner but in a remote manner, to mystical contemplation considered as a normal flowering of the grace of the theological virtues and of the gifts of the Holy Spirit—a thesis

[3] Garrigou-Lagrange, loc. cit.
[4] La Doctrine Spirituelle, éd. Pottier (Paris: Téqui, 1936), pp. 430–2.

in line with Christian tradition and with the spiritual teaching of Saint Bonaventure and of Saint Thomas—has been masterfully expounded by Father Garrigou-Lagrange.[5] And to the extent that it is well understood—we mean, with all the nuances and all the adjustments which it requires—it is, despite some passing opposition, well on the way to becoming classical.

As to "the proximate call to the mystical life," it "exists only when the three signs mentioned by Saint John of the Cross, and before him by Tauler are clearly present: 1) meditation becomes impossible; 2) the soul has no desire to fix the imagination on any particular object, interior or exterior; 3) the soul delights in finding itself alone with God, fixing on Him its loving attention." [6]

---

[5] Especially in *Perfection chrétienne et Contemplation,* often cited in this study, and in *L'Amour de Dieu et la Croix de Jésus.* See also the article in *Dictionnaire de Spiritualité,* t. II (Paris: Beauchesne, 1953), "La Contemplation dans l'école dominicaine," col. 2067–2079, in which Father Garrigou-Lagrange has condensed his teaching on contemplation.

[6] Garrigou-Lagrange, *Perfection chrétienne et Contemplation,* t. II, pp. 421–2.

CHAPTER II

*Either typical or masked forms of contemplation
"The prayer of the heart"*

We have said that all souls are called, at least in
a remote manner, to the mystical life, that is to
say, to life under the regime of the gifts of the
Holy Spirit.

"We must now observe that among the inspir-
ing gifts which Catholic theology has learned
from Isaias to enumerate, some, like the gifts of
Counsel, Fortitude and Fear of the Lord, relate
especially to action; others, like the gifts of Understanding and Wisdom, relate especially to
contemplation.

"It follows that souls which have entered into
the way of the spirit will be able to travel it in very
different ways and according to extremely different styles. With some it is the highest gifts, the
gifts of Wisdom and Understanding, which are exercised to a high degree; these souls represent mys-

tical life in its normal plenitude, and they will have the grace of contemplation in its typical forms, be they arid or consoling. With others it is the other gifts which are exercised above all; [7] these souls will live a mystical life, but chiefly as to their activities and their works, and they will not have the typical and normal forms of contemplation.

"It is not however that they are deprived of contemplation, of the loving experience of divine things; for according to the teaching of Saint Thomas all the gifts of the Holy Spirit are connected (*Sum. theol.*, I–II, 68, 5), they cannot therefore exist in a soul without the gift of Wisdom, which, in the case we are speaking of, is exercised still, although in a less apparent way. Those souls whose style of life is active will have the grace of contemplation, but of a *masked* and unapparent contemplation; perhaps they will be capable only of reciting rosaries, and mental

---

[7] Cf. J. and R. Maritain, *De la vie d'oraison,* Nouvelle éd. revue et corrigée (Paris: Rouart, 1947), Note IV.

Infused contemplation, Father Garrigou-Lagrange writes, "very manifest in the perfect ones who are more inclined to the contemplative life, is, as it were, diffuse in the other perfect ones in whom chiefly predominate the gifts of the Holy Ghost relative to action—the gifts of Fear of the Lord, Fortitude, Counsel, Knowledge, united to the gift of Piety, under a less visible influence of the gifts of Wisdom and Understanding." *Op. cit.,* I, p. 214.

prayer will bring them only a headache or sleep. Mysterious contemplation will not be in their conscious prayer, but perhaps in the glance with which they will look at a poor man, or look at suffering." [8]

We have just insisted on the diffuse or disguised forms of infused contemplation. There is nothing more secret—nor more important—than what Father Osende, in a remarkable page of his book *Contemplata*,[9] calls the prayer of the heart. It is through this sort of prayer or contemplation, so silent and so rooted in the depths of the spirit that he describes it as "unconscious," that we can truly put into practice the precept to pray *always*. And it is not to it that Saint Anthony the hermit alluded when he said that "there is no perfect prayer if the religious perceives that he is praying"? [10]

"We must observe," writes Father Osende,

[8] Cf. Jacques Maritain, "Action et Contemplation," in *Questions de Conscience* (Paris: Desclée De Brouwer, 1938), pp. 144–6. According to Saint Bonaventure, all the gifts, "each in its place, facilitate mystical experience because they purify, illumine and perfect" (Ephrem Longpré, *Dict. de Spiritualité,* col. 2083).

[9] Translated into English under the title *Fruits of Contemplation* (St. Louis: Herder, 1953).

[10] "Non est perfecta oratio in qua se monachus vel hoc ipsum quod orat intelligit." Cassian, IX, 31. Let us note that the idea of perpetual or continuous prayer, which is prolonged even into sleep by a subconscious mental activity, plays a central role in Cassian. (Cf. *Dict. de Spiritualité,* article on Contemplation, col. 1924 and 1926.)

"that prayer can be of two kinds: prayer of the
mind and prayer of the heart or of the spirit. . . .
Both, of course, can be practiced at the same time.
Prayer of the mind . . . requires all our attention
and care and the actual exercise of our faculties.
Such prayer cannot be continuous in this life. . . .

"The prayer of the heart or of the spirit (which
we shall call 'unconscious' prayer because it is
made without reflection and without our attention's being actually fixed on it) can and should
be continuous throughout one's life. The reason
for this distinction is that, although we cannot fix
our mind on two things at the same time nor con-
tinue to think always, we can love always. . . .

"What does it matter if our mind and senses are
occupied with a thousand different things? Our
heart is elsewhere, fixed on God, so that everything we do and think, we do through Him, in
Him and for Him. . . . Who does not see that this
is possible, and very possible? Do we not see that,
even in the natural order, when the heart is domi-
nated by a great love, no matter what the person
does, his entire soul and life are on what he loves
and not on what he does, though he may apply to
his work all his mind and attention? If natural

love does this, how much more should divine love. . . .

"He who practices unconscious prayer in all its plenitude, that is, he who has attained the state of constant prayer, finds that his heart is almost constantly recollected in God and divine things, for his spirit draws him irresistibly toward the divine and eternal and his heart is drawn to where his treasure lies. Hence Saint John of the Cross says (*Ascent of Mount Carmel,* III, 26): 'To him that is pure, all things, whether high or low . . . all the operations of the senses and faculties are directed to divine contemplation. Such a man . . . finds in all things a knowledge of God which is joyful and pleasant, chaste, pure, spiritual, glad and loving.' " [11]

---

[11] Victorino Osende, *Fruits of Contemplation,* pp. 157–9. Father Grou, in the 18th century, had already noted (*Manuel,* pp. 224 ss.) that continuous prayer is a prayer which escapes consciousness. See Arintero, *the Mystical Evolution in the Development and Vitality of the Church,* Vol. II (St. Louis: Herder, 1951), p. 45. This idea is already indicated by Cassian.

CHAPTER III

Contemplation and the call to perfection

Dominating the whole spiritual life is the call to perfection.

"Be you therefore perfect, as also your heavenly Father is perfect." [12]

"Christian perfection consists essentially in charity," says Saint Thomas.[13] "Indeed a thing is said to be perfect in so far as it attains its proper end—the proper end of a thing being its ultimate perfection. Now it is charity that unites us to God, Who is the last end of the human soul: *he that abideth in charity, abideth in God, and God in him.*" [14]

It follows that perfection falls under the divine precept, because it is on charity, on the twofold love of God and neighbor, that the two precepts of the divine Law bear.

[12] Matt. 5:48.
[13] *Sum. theol.*, II–II, 184, 1 and 3.
[14] *Ibid.*, 184, 1.

And "the love of God and of neighbor does not fall under the precept according to a certain measure only . . . as is evident from the very form of the precept, which implies perfection and totality: 'Thou shalt love the Lord thy God with thy whole heart, thy whole soul, thy whole mind, thy whole strength, and thy neighbor as thyself.' This is why the Apostle says (I *Tim.*, 1): *the end of the commandment is charity*. Now the end does not admit of measure—measure applies only to means." [15]

According to Saint Bernard's saying, the measure of loving God is to love Him without measure—*modus diligendi, sine modo diligere*.

Estote perfecti. "Thus the Lord in His goodness," says Saint Benedict, commenting on this word of Christ's in the prologue to his Rule, "shows us the way of life"—the way of eternal life, which must never be interrupted, so that charity may grow unceasingly, at the same time as humility which is the dawn of beatitude—*incipit beatitudo ab humilitate*.

The way of life which Christ shows us is a way in which one advances towards God and towards the Beatific Vision with steps of living faith, of hope, and of love. And because it makes one ad-

[15] *Ibid.*, 184, 3.

vance towards perfection, this way itself is perfect.

Perfection is not a mathematical point. It is a life in state of growth; there are degrees in perfection. What is prescribed by the precept is to tend to perfection as to an end, and when one has begun to make his way towards it he is already accomplishing the precept; and one begins to make his way towards it as soon as he has charity. It is in this sense that Saint Thomas tells us: "Since what falls under the precept can be accomplished in diverse ways, one does not sin against the precept by the fact alone that he does not fulfil it in the best way; it suffices, for the precept not to be transgressed, that it be accomplished in one way or another." [16] And Cajetan writes: "The perfection of charity is commanded as an end; and we must wish to attain the end, the whole end. But precisely because it is an end, it suffices, for a man not to transgress the precept, that he be in the state of attaining this perfection one day, even if in eternity. Whoever possesses charity, even in the feeblest degree, and is thus advancing towards Heaven, is in the way of perfect charity, and consequently avoids the transgression of the precept. . . ." [17]

[16] *Ibid.*, 184, 3, ad 2.
[17] Cajetan, *in II–II*, 184, 3.

It is only in Heaven where the soul sees God face to face that the precept is accomplished in an entirely perfect way. But there is a perfection of charity compatible with the present life, a perfection in state of growth; it implies "the exclusion of all things which are repugnant to the movement of love towards God"—the exclusion not only of mortal sin, but also of "all that hinders the affection of the soul from tending entirely towards God." [18] And thus, whatever may be the vocation of each, the saying of Saint John of the Cross concerns us all: *In the evening of this life you will be judged according to your love.*

*

Let us recall now that contemplation, as Father Lallemant puts it, "proceeds from love and tends to love," that it is "the use of the purest and most perfect charity," and that love is "its source, its exercise and its end"—as indeed Saint Paul affirmed, for whom charity—in the words of Father Lebreton—which "at death will flower into eternal life," [19] is "the way and the end of contemplation." [20] And let us recall too that according to the teaching of Saint Thomas contemplation

[18] *Sum. theol.,* II–II, 184, 2.
[19] *Dict. de Spiritualité,* col. 1715.
[20] *Ibid.,* col. 1711.

"relates directly and immediately to the love of God Himself," [21] and that it "is ordered not to any love of God whatever, but to perfect love." [22] What are we to conclude from all this if not that the precept of perfection protects, so to speak, and sanctions the desire for contemplation: there is no true contemplation without progress towards perfection; and on the other hand there is nothing which accelerates better than contemplation one's progress towards perfection and the accomplishment in us of the desire for perfection.

[21] *Sum. theol.*, 182, 2.
[22] *Ibid.*, 182, 4, ad 1.

CHAPTER IV

A question which should be divided into two different ones

It is important here—in order to avoid possible misunderstandings—that we be as precise as possible about these things.

It is sometimes asked if there is a real link between the plenitude of Christian perfection and "higher infused contemplation." [23]

We believe that the question as posed in this way cannot receive from the data of experience a simple answer. Indeed the answer is twofold. What seems to follow from experience is, in the first place, that higher infused contemplation seems to be always linked to a high perfection; but is, in the second place, that high perfection does not seem to be always linked to higher infused contemplation, in the sense of the typical forms expounded by the masters.

---

[23] Cf. Charles Baumgartner, article on Contemplation, "Conclusion générale," *Dict. de Spiritualité,* col. 2183.

This absence of symmetry precludes any agreement among theologians on this question so long as the two different questions it involves are not distinguished from each other.

But in reality the difficulty comes above all from the fact that the question in the form in which it is posed does not take into account the freedom of the Spirit of God, Who does as He likes with the souls He wants to unite to Himself.

The question is not to know if the summit of the perfection of love coincides necessarily with the summit of mystical contemplation in its typical and fully unfolded state. The question is to know if, on the one hand, it is necessary that the soul, in order to attain to infused contemplation, decidedly makes its way, despite its weaknesses, towards the perfection of charity and full purification; and if, on the other hand, in order to attain to the perfection of love, it is necessary for it to enter in one way or another (typical or atypical, open or masked) into the ways of infused contemplation—which comes to saying that infused contemplation, to one degree or another and under one form or another, is in the normal way of sanctity.

To the question posed in these terms, it seems

clear to us—as will appear in a more developed manner in the pages following—that the answer must be in the affirmative. And we do not think it rash to think that this affirmative answer falls into the category of the assertions on which Father Baumgartner rightly judges that every one should be in agreement.[24]

[24] Cf. *ibid.*, col. 2182–2183.

CHAPTER V

Contemplation to one degree or another, even though diffuse or masked, is in the normal way of perfection

The saints realize to perfection the commandment to love God and neighbor. And it is because they love God with the best of their hearts and with all their strength, that they are in general great contemplatives, and in some way always contemplatives. As Saint Bonaventure constantly insists, Christ Himself promised them this experience of divine things when He said in Saint John (14:21): "He that loveth me, shall be loved by my Father: and I will love him, and will manifest myself to him."

Sanctity is the full perfection of the soul, and perfection is to love God without measure. But contemplation is directly ordered to union with God, and union with God proceeds from the perfection of love.

Thus perfection and contemplation are normally linked by reason of charity, on which they both depend; and contemplation, even if diffuse and masked, is the hidden manna on which the soul must normally nourish itself—through all the trials of life, and in order to establish itself fully in the love of God and neighbor.

Vacate et videte quoniam ego sum Deus; be still and see that I am God, it is said in Psalm 45. It is thus that contemplation calls us, and that God calls us to contemplation. "Taste and see that the Lord is sweet." [25]

How could man come to the perfection of charity if he did not keep himself habitually in the presence of God, and did not tend with his whole heart to being united with Him? The search for perfection disposes one to contemplation, and contemplation, by increasing the perfection of love, increases the perfection of the virtues.

"Without contemplation," writes Father Lallemant, "one will never make much progress in virtue. . . . One will never entirely get out of his weaknesses and his imperfections. One will always be attached to the earth, and will never rise much above the sentiments of nature. Never will one

[25] *Gustave et videte quoniam suavis est Dominus* (Ps. 33).

render to God a perfect service. But with it one will do more in a month, both for himself and for others, than one would do without it in ten years. It produces . . . most sublime acts of love of God, which one only very rarely makes without this gift . . . and finally it perfects faith and all the virtues . . ." [26]

Thus there is continuity between ascetical doctrine and mystical doctrine—spiritual doctrine is one. Ascetical doctrine must begin by showing "the end to which spiritual progress must tend, that is to say, Christian perfection . . . in all its grandeur, according to the testimony of the Gospel and of the saints." [27] And asceticism does not cease when the soul enters into the mystical union. "To the very end the soul must remember the words of Our Lord: *If anyone wishes to come after me, let him deny himself and take up his cross daily.*" [28]

[26] *La Doctrine Spirituelle*, pp. 429–30.
[27] Garrigou-Lagrange, *op. cit.*, t. I, p. 39.
[28] *Ibid.*

CHAPTER VI

Contemplation and the gifts of the Holy Spirit

We have just seen that perfection and contemplation imply each other by reason of love which is at once the essence of perfection and "the source, the exercise and the end" of contemplation. One can also show this mutual implication by stressing the fact that life under the regime of the gifts of the Holy Spirit is the state proper to perfection and to contemplation all at once.

Saint Thomas teaches that the gifts of the Holy Spirit are necessary for salvation, because we are too weak all by ourselves always to use as we should even the theological virtues and the infused moral virtues.[29] There is much greater reason to say that the gifts of the Holy Spirit are necessary for perfection. The sons of God are moved by the spirit of God,[30] the perfect live under the regime

[29] Cf. *Sum. theol.*, I, 68, 2.
[30] *Quicumque spiritu Dei aguntur, ii sunt filii Dei* (St. Paul, Rom. 8:14).

of the gifts of the Spirit. But to enter under the regime of the gifts of the Spirit is precisely to cross the threshold of infused contemplation.[31] For, as Saint Bonaventure tells us, "the gifts immediately dispose one to contemplation." [32]

Without some form or other of habitual contemplation, would it be possible for the soul effectively to perceive, in the midst of afflictions and torments, that "the duties of each moment," as Father de Caussade put it, "conceal, under their obscure appearances, the truth of the divine will," and that "they are as it were the sacraments of the present moment"? Commenting on Saint Paul's words, "the Spirit helpeth our infirmity . . ." [33] the great Carmelite theologian Thomas of Jesus writes: "These words clearly refer to the particular motion or aid of the Holy Spirit, and point to the need that we have of it. . . . It is the gifts of the Holy Spirit which make the soul promptly docile, entirely free, capable of overcoming difficulties,

[31] Cf. the masterful treatise of John of Saint-Thomas, *Les Dons du Saint-Esprit*, French translation by Raïssa Maritain (Paris: Cerf, 1930; 2° éd. Téqui, 1950); English translation by Father Dominic Hughes, O.P. (New York: Sheed and Ward, 1951).

[32] Cf. Ephrem Longpré, *Dict. de Spiritualité*, col. 2083.

[33] "The Spirit also helpeth our infirmity. For we know what we should pray for as we ought; but the Spirit himself asketh for us with unspeakable groanings. And he that searcheth the hearts, knoweth what the Spirit desireth; because he asketh for the saints according to God" (Rom. 8:26–7).

and wholly occupied with God in prayer and contemplation. This effect cannot be produced even
by the infused virtue of religion, nor by the theological virtues by themselves." [34] This is as much
as to say that the life of perfection is an inspired
life, and therefore a life which—perhaps in secret
—infused contemplation nourishes and sustains.

[34] Venerable Thomas of Jesus, *De Oratione divina*, I, 2.

CHAPTER VII

The tradition of the saints

We can conclude that in his fine study on the mystical theology of Saint Bonaventure, it is not only the teaching of Saint Bonaventure but the whole tradition of the saints that Father Ephrem Longpré summarizes, when he writes: "the contemplative state is only the supreme blooming of the supernatural life, the positively experienced flowering of grace and the infused habits, the higher exercise of the gifts of the Holy Spirit. . . . By a necessary consequence, the mystical life is the ordinary way of perfection." [35]

[35] Ephrem Longpré, *La théologie mystique de saint Bonaventure,* in "Archivum Franciscanum Historicum," 1921, fasc. I and II. Cf. the articles of Father Longpré on Saint Bonaventure (*Dict. de Spiritualité,* col. 1777–1791), and on contemplation in the Franciscan school (*ibid.,* article on Contemplation, col. 2080–2102). According to Saint Bonaventure, he writes, "there exists a promise of mystical or Christian experience; everything is disposed . . . so that Christ's pledge (John, XIV, 21) may be realized with full right in every believer in whom the Holy Trinity dwells and who fulfils the required conditions: the observance of the commandments and the love of Christ Jesus" (col. 2080). "The Gospel makes neither distinction nor exception; it mentions

Saint Bonaventure and his contemporary Saint Thomas Aquinas,[36] those two great representatives of theology and mysticism in the thirteenth century, were not however saints of the reflex age! Nor were Saint Irenaeus, Saint Gregory of Nyssa, Evagrius, Saint Ambrose, Saint Augustine, Diadochus, Saint Gregory the Great, Saint John Climacus, Maximus the Confessor, Saint Bernard, Hugh of Saint Victor, the Carthusian Guiges du Chastel, Saint Hildegard, Saint Albert the Great, Saint Gertrude, Angela of Foligno, Tauler, Suso, Saint Catherine of Siena, the author of the *Cloud of Unknowing,* Ruysbroeck the Admirable. . . .

In the fifth century, Cassian, transmitting in his *Conferences* the lessons of spirituality which he had received from the Fathers of the Desert,

---

no privilege, it requires no other vocation than the Christian life: *He that loveth me, shall be loved of my Father: and I will love him, and will manifest myself to him* (John, XIV, 21)." (Col. 2096.)

[36] The spiritual teaching of Saint Thomas Aquinas is summed up excellently in columns 1983–1988 of Father Paul Phillipe's article on contemplation in the thirteenth century (*Dict. de Spiritualité*). Let us note the following remarks (col. 1986): "It properly belongs to infused wisdom to increase by itself the love of God in the soul. . . . Mystical contemplation is wholly impregnated by love and cannot not give rise to a greater love." And if from love knowledge can proceed, it is *"because charity enables one to judge well of the things of God: such is the science of the saints* (Saint Thomas, *in Phil.,* c. 1, lect. 2)"—in which love causes the intelligence to enter "into the depths of God" in virtue of a knowledge by affinity under the motion of the Holy Spirit.

teaches that the Lord Himself placed the "principal good" in divine contemplation, a spiritual science accorded to purity of heart—and to charity —by the illumination of the Holy Spirit. For him contemplation is a light inseparable from moral purity. Without moral purity, no contemplation is possible. At the highest moments supervenes the "prayer of fire," provoked by an operation of the Holy Spirit which he compares to a puff of wind on a light feather, and in which love ravishes the soul in an ineffable experience, light in the mind and flame in the will.[37]

In the following century, Saint Gregory the Great, "the most eminent spiritual author in the West up to the end of the Middle Ages," [38] continues and adds to the tradition which Cassian had echoed. The higher the soul rises, the more it tends to contemplate "the beauty of our Creator in a knowledge through love, *per amorem agnoscimus.*" [39]

"There is not for faithful souls," he writes,[40]

[37] Cf. Michel Olphe-Galliard, article on Contemplation, *Dict. de Spiritualité,* col. 1921–1929.

[38] Jean Leclercq, article on Contemplation, *Dict. de Spiritualité,* col. 1933.

[39] R. Gillet, *Introduction aux Homélies morales sur Job* (Paris, 1951), p. 32. Cf. *Moralia* X, 8, 13.

[40] In *Ezechiel,* II, Hom. 5. Cited by Garrigou-Lagrange, *op. cit.,* p. 675.

"any function which is incompatible with the grace of contemplation; every truly interior man can be graced with its lights, and no one can glory in them as in an extraordinary privilege." Saint Gregory also noted—as Saint Bernard was to do—the painful passive purifications which Saint John of the Cross later called the nights of the senses and of the spirit.[41]

Prayer seeks, contemplation finds, said Hugh of Saint Victor; and Tauler: "The soul, leaving aside every useless external occupation, will find through the abnegation of its own will and true humility a certain quietude and supernatural experience of divine things, which leads to full perfection, in which one has a supernatural view of everything. . . ." [42]

Dom Huyben has shown [43] that "the doctrine of the normal, though eminent, character of the mystical life is admitted by Saint Bernard, Tauler, Louis de Blois, and that no one contradicted it in the Middle Ages." [44] The idea that mystical contemplation is the normal flowering of the graces of the perfect life was common doctrine.

[41] Cf. Garrigou-Lagrange, *op. cit.,* pp. 675 and 684.
[42] *Ibid.,* pp. 686 and 694, note 2.
[43] In a remarkable article on "La Tradition mystique au moyen âge," *Vie Spirituelle,* January, 1922, pp. 298 ss.
[44] Garrigou-Lagrange, *op. cit.,* p. 690.

*

To sum everything up, let us say that the source of contemplation is the constant search for the greater and greater perfection of the soul, and that perfection consists essentially in charity; and that it is also on the love of God that contemplation lives. The most pure desire of God is therefore essential to it. The great contemplatives of all ages, those of the reflex age as also those prior to the reflex age, desire only God alone.

"I do not count myself for anything," says Saint Hildegard in the twelfth century. . . . "I turn towards the living God in order that He may deign in all things to keep me from evil."

"What do my concerns matter, Lord," exclaims Saint Teresa of Avila. "For me there is no longer anything but You."

PART THREE

AGAINST SOME MISCONCEP-
TIONS WHICH TEND TO
DIVERT CHRISTIAN SOULS
FROM CONTEMPLATION

CHAPTER I

So-called techniques to lead us to union with God?

How is it possible that the truths recalled in the preceding pages, and which are an integral part of the venerable heritage of the Doctors of the Church and of the Saints, are put in question by some who, presenting themselves as the barristers of the Sacred Liturgy itself, reprove, in the name of the public prayer of the Church, mental prayer, solitude with God, and silent contemplation?

Those who take such a position do not know what contemplation is and they misunderstand the Sacred Liturgy. They do not know that these two supernatural realities and grandeurs must be associated and not divided.

Need we bring up some of the grievances which the detractors of solitary prayer and of contemplation advance?

One sometimes hears it said that whereas the collective movement of the liturgy draws us of itself and quite spontaneously towards God, the masters who teach us the ways of meditation, of infused prayer and of contemplative union, propose to the efforts of each one systematic formulas and techniques to be applied. We have here a strange misunderstanding. Ascetical and mystical science teaches us to liberate ourselves from the obstacles which are in us, so that we may be able to let the gifts of grace act freely in our soul. But it teaches us at the same time to hold for an illusion every effort to attain perfection and contemplative union by any kind of systematic procedure, formula or technique. As concerns infused contemplation in particular, is not the essential fact, as we recalled in the preceding section, that it coincides with the entry of the soul under the regime of the gifts of the Holy Spirit?

"What is it to say this, if not that Christian contemplation depends above all on that Spirit who breathes where He wills, and whose voice one hears, yet without anyone knowing whence He comes or whither He goes . . . (John, III, 8). This means that Christian contemplation is quite the contrary of a matter of *technique*. . . ." [1] Natural spirituality, like that of India for example,

[1] J. Maritain, *Questions de conscience,* p. 149.

has quite fixed techniques. "This apparatus of techniques is what first strikes one who begins to study comparative mysticism. Well, one of the most obvious differences between Christian mysticism and other mysticisms is its liberty as regards technique, as regards all recipes and formulae . . ." [2] "It is necessary," writes Father Osende,[3] "to affirm once and for all, in accordance with the doctrine of the Church and the saints, that there is no method, procedure, or rule whereby one may acquire or induce mystical contemplation. All that we can do is to dispose ourselves so that God will communicate it to us when it pleases Him."

[2] J. Maritain, *loc. cit.*
[3] *Op. cit.*, p. 176.

CHAPTER II

A so-called "subjective" and egocentric spirituality?

One also hears formulated sometimes another series of grievances: ascetical preparations, solitary meditation, the desire for and the experience of infused prayer, all this—some say—arises from a spirituality in which the soul is turned towards itself and seeks itself. Under pretext of seeking mystical union it abandons itself to introspection and to a psychological fixation on its own interior states, in which a disguised egoism holds the first place and which many a time would call for the attentions of the psychologist or psychoanalyst rather than of the spiritual director. To this spirituality that one terms "subjective," one opposes then the purely "objective" and entirely disinterested spirituality of the liturgy, which in convoking the whole of creation to the praise of God and in absorbing each one in the prayer and the élan of the assembly of the faithful, cures the soul of egoistic seeking of self and teaches it to be contented with honoring God through the worship which is rendered to Him in common.

It is true that liturgical prayer is a precious aid to contemplative souls, in particular in their effort to deliver themselves from the complications and returns on self to which our psychological mechanisms naturally incline us. Apart from this, it must be said that under beautiful phrases on the liturgy the kind of talk to which we have alluded contains serious errors. In the encyclical *Mediator Dei*, Pope Pius XII refutes a so-called purely "objective" spirituality which would exclude all "subjective" spirituality, in other words, which would exclude all spirituality in which the person as such is engaged in his unique relation with God.[4]

Before going any further, it is perhaps not irrelevant to cite the lines in which Monsignor Knox expressed with smiling British reserve some very wise remarks: "We have been using mental prayer for years, and it doesn't seem to have made much difference to our characters; have we any reason to think that this form of worship is specially pleasing to God?

[4] Cf. *Mediator Dei*, pp. 13–15.

"To that objection, I have only a word to say, which I will leave with you; I may be quite wrong. I think mental prayer is imperative, if only to plough up the mind and leave it fallow for God's inspirations. He may want to tell you about something you are meant to do for Him; and although He does not need our help in creating the opportunity for Him, it seems to me that we are wrong if we do not create it. All the masses and all the office we say can leave His voice unheard; we shout it down with our importunities." [5]

But let us consider now the true bearing and the internal logic of things. Behind the criticisms addressed to the seeking of self supposedly implied in the practice of meditation and the docility to the mystical ways, it is to be feared that there is found simply the desire to escape from the demands which God causes to be heard within, and from that total gift of oneself through which He brings it about that finally a soul is no longer but "a single spirit and love" with Him. To honor God through worship rendered in common and through the virtue of religion is, we recalled above, the highest thing in the order of the moral virtues. But

[5] Ronald Knox, in his posthumous book, *The Priestly Life: Conference on Prayer* (New York: Sheed and Ward, 1958), p. 131.

one cannot impose on souls that they stop their aspirations there, nor that they use such a noble good to turn them aside from a still higher good, which belongs directly to the theological virtues and the gifts of the Holy Spirit, and in which the very love of God for the creatures He made to His image is concerned.

No one denies that a psychological fixation on oneself, even an unhealthy anxiety for introspection, can mingle with piety, even sincere piety, in many souls. But the masters of asceticism are the first to denounce the illusions caused by these parasites. It is absurd to reproach mental prayer and interior recollection with what is their counterfeit. It being a fact that infused contemplation exists only through the love of God sovereignly loved, and only for that, it is pure nonsense to accuse of a kind of transcendent egoism those to whom it gives in reality only a supreme desire: *cupio dissolvi et esse cum Christo*—"I desire to be dissolved and to be with Christ."

To be anxious about one's own perfection (according to the spirit of Christianity, let us understand) implies no egoist seeking of self, for it is for the love of God, not of one's self, that the Christian aspires to become perfect. It is clear besides that one could not advance in the love of God if he were not constantly attentive to conquering himself and to purifying himself of all that which within him constitutes an obstacle to charity. There comes however a moment—when the soul has progressed rather far in the way of the spirit— when, through the effect of the contemplative union itself, concern for one's own perfection, as necessary as it may remain, passes into the background. Then the soul no longer thinks of anything but loving. With those who have reached this stage, holy preoccupation—centered in God, not in self—with one's own perfection ceases to attract the attention of conscious thought.

"They are no longer preoccupied with self, but only with the extension of the Kingdom of God throughout the world, that His name may be loved and glorified by all men, beginning with themselves. All their prayers, petitions, works, and sacrifices are directed principally toward this end and they are converted into invisible channels through which the graces of heaven descend upon earth." [6] Thus it is by virtue of contemplation that the supreme degree of forgetfulness of self is attained.

[6] Victorino Osende, *op. cit.,* p. 310. This whole page could well be cited.

"Contemplation alone," we wrote elsewhere, "discovers the value of charity. Without it, one knows it by hearsay; with it, one knows it by experience. Through love and in love, it makes known that God is love. Then man lets God do in him what He wills; he lets himself be bound because he loves; he is free because he loves. All that has not the taste of love loses for him all savor. Because of that love, with which it perfects our life, contemplation alone realizes in us universality, renders the soul catholic in spirit and in truth. As it transcends all the intellectual and moral virtues, prudence, science and art, so also it transcends all particularisms, attunes the soul to the unity of the Mystical Body. . . . Through it, Christ, dwelling in those who love Him, gives their hearts a sort of Eucharistic amplitude." [7]

[7] J. Maritain, *Primauté du Spirituel,* pp. 171–172.

CHAPTER III

The saints of the reflex age

There is a last argument to which those who would like to reject the authority of Saint John of the Cross and of Saint Teresa readily have recourse. It is drawn from the diversity of ages in history. Saint Teresa and Saint John of the Cross, they say, were saints of the reflex age. They probably had to write as they did, given their historical epoch. What they wrote was probably good for that age of history, but it has no value for our age, which has suffered only too much from individual introspection and whose essential need is in the social and communal order.

Such a reasoning contains many errors. The fundamental error consists in forgetting that if there are in the spiritual life a development and modalities which are linked with the movement of history, the substance itself of this life depends neither on time nor on history but on supratemporal truths. Why is it that one does not see that it is essentially the same doctrine which, taught in the sixteenth century by Saint John of the Cross in the perspective of the practical science of the spiritual life, was taught in the thirteenth century by Saint Thomas Aquinas and Saint Bonaventure in the perspective of theology? Why does one forget the teachings of the Fathers and of the medieval Doctors on the primacy of contemplation, the decisive importance of which we stressed above? And why does one forget the mysterious continuity in which, in the *Living Flame of Love* of Saint John of the Cross, the *darkness* of Saint Gregory of Nyssa finally recognizes its true nature? By what strange blindness does one fail to recognize the testimony given by the saints and the great spiritual writers, all through the Christian centuries, to that very experience of the depths of God whose states and degrees Saint Teresa and Saint John of the Cross only succeeded in describing in a more analytical and more explicit manner?

It is true that with Saint Teresa and Saint John of the Cross (and with Saint Francis of Sales also) there was an explicit and reflexive *prise de conscience* of what takes place at the interior of the soul that has entered into the contemplative way.

For such a growth in awareness there was required—given its object—a special gift of God,
the grace of a high supernatural light received for
the enlightening of the whole Church. Such a
growth in awareness constituted of itself an immense progress. It apprised us of the precious
treasures which at the most secret depths of the
soul we hold from the life of grace. Doubtless, as
with every growth in awareness, it was accompanied by accidental dangers. But of itself, as with
every growth in awareness, it obeyed—and in the
purest and highest domain—the very law of the
spirit and of the growth of the spirit. It is not a
gesture of the hands by way of taking leave of
them more or less courteously, it is an incomparable gratitude that we owe—and shall always owe
—to the great saints of the reflex age.

It is true also that our historical age has other
needs than that of Saint Teresa and Saint John of
the Cross. But it is certainly not in the aspiration
to submit everything to the primacy of the social
and the communal that these true needs of our
age are to be sought. As concerns the spiritual life
in particular, the true and authentic need of our
age is, on the one hand, to understand better the
mystery of the Mystical Body (which transcends

to the infinite the natural social and the human communal); and it is, on the other hand, and especially, to understand—without losing or neglecting anything of the teaching of the masters on contemplation—that today contemplation asks, we do not say to leave the cloisters and the convents, but to go out of doors and spread its wings, and to have done with the illusion, too frequent among people, that it should be reserved for specialists. "As soon as a man is fully disposed to be alone with God, he is alone with God no matter where he may be—in the country, the monastery, the woods or the city." [8]

[8] Thomas Merton, *Thoughts in Solitude* (New York: Farrar, Straus and Cudahy, 1958), p. 96.

CHAPTER IV

Contemplation on the roads of the world

Indeed contemplation is not given only to the Carthusians, the Poor Clares, the Carmelites. . . . It is frequently the treasure of persons hidden in the world, known only to some few—to their directors, to a few friends. Sometimes, in a certain manner this treasure is hidden from the souls themselves who possess it—souls who live by it in all simplicity, without visions, without miracles, but with such a flame of love for God and neighbor that good happens all around them without noise and without agitation.

It is of this that our age has to become aware, and of the ways through which contemplation communicates itself through the world, under one form or the other, to the great multitude of souls who thirst for it (often without knowing it), and who are called to it at least in a remote manner. The great need of our age, in what concerns the

spiritual life, is to put contemplation on the roads
of the world.

It is fitting to note here the importance of the
witness and the mission of Saint Thérèse of
Lisieux. It would be futile to seek an opposition
between her and Saint John of the Cross, whom
she called "the saint of Love par excellence." In
substance it is the same spirituality, but everything has undergone in her a marvelous reduction
to the essential. Not only all the extraordinary
graces to which Saint John of the Cross forbade
the soul to aspire and to attach itself, but all the
great typical signs, terrible or resplendent, which
manifested, in the soul's own experience, the
stages traversed by it in advancing in the way of
union—all these things have now disappeared.
There is in Saint Thérèse of Lisieux—and with an
unbelievably pure limpidity—no longer anything
but total love, total gift, and total stripping of
self. It is a great way indeed, this *petite voie* of
Thérèse's—and an heroic one—but one which
hides rigorously its grandeur under an absolute
simplicity, itself heroic. And this absolute simplicity makes of it a way *par excellence* open to all
those who aspire to perfection, whatever their condition of life may be. This is the feature here that

it is particularly important for us to keep in mind.

Saint Thérèse of the Infant Jesus has shown that the soul can tend to the perfection of charity by a way in which the great signs that Saint John of the Cross and Saint Teresa of Avila described, and which find themselves in preference in convents, do not appear. At the same stroke, we believe, Saint Thérèse in her Carmel prepared in an eminent way that wider diffusion than ever of the life of union with God which the world requires if it is not to perish.

Let us add that in this contemplation "on the roads of the world," whose development the future will doubtless witness, it seems that constant attention to the presence of Jesus and fraternal charity are called to play a major role, as regards even the ways of infused prayer. We believe that the vocation of those contemplatives thrown into the world and the misery of the world who are the Little Brothers of Charles de Foucauld, has in this respect a high significance, and that one can expect from them new lights in the domain of the spiritual life, with time and the grace of God.

CHAPTER V

The liturgy transcends essentially every natural aspiration for community

Liturgical worship, we have already noted, is an end in itself; but it tends by nature to prepare and to lead those who participate in it to a higher end, which is contemplation. To claim to deprive the liturgy of this ordination to contemplation, is to denature the liturgy. "One point we stress over and over," says Father Alfred C. Longley, pastor of St. Richard's in Minneapolis, one of the most remarkable liturgical parishes in the United States, "is that the aim of worship—through Mass and the sacraments—is love." [9] Why then should not participation in the liturgical service tend to prepare us for that contemplative union in which the perfection of love for God and for all men normally takes root? Those who turn souls aside from contemplation in the name of the liturgy are, con-

[9] Cf. *Jubilee*, No. cited, p. 40.

trary to what they think, great enemies of the liturgy itself. Such a disregard for mental prayer and contemplation certainly does not arise from a true view of the liturgy, but on what it is fitting to call a "pseudo-liturgical systematization."

We said just now that one of the great needs of our age is to understand better the mystery of the Mystical Body. It is this need that is being met by the effort of all those, priests and laymen, who dedicate themselves with an admirable zeal to the liturgical renewal, thereby restoring so many parishes to an authentic life and to a common fervor in worship worthily rendered, and helping the faithful to realize better, through their union with the public prayer of the Church, their belonging to the Mystical Body.[10]

It is to an essentially supernatural society—in which we are "fellow-citizens of the saints," and whose principle of life, invisible to our bodily eyes, is the Blood of Christ and the grace of the Holy Ghost—that we thus realize better our belonging. What is essentially important, and what we have

[10] It is to be noted—and this is entirely normal—that many advocates of the liturgical renewal are at the same time fervent defenders of the mystical life and of contemplation. Such is the case, for example, with Father H. A. Reinhold (cf. his two books, *The American Parish and the Roman Liturgy* [New York: Macmillan, 1958] and *Soul Afire* [New York: Pantheon Books, 1944]).

to actualize in our entire life, is the typically supernatural quality which makes us members of the Mystical Body and of the communion of saints. This is clearly quite another thing from being a member of a choir, although the singing of the choir is a part of the public prayer of the Church, and although it depends on our interior fervor that our singing be an act of love elevating our soul towards God.

Let us add that in understanding better the divine social life of the Church and our belonging to the Mystical Body we are normally drawn to understand better also the authentic exigencies of the human social life and the necessity of making fraternal love prevail in it. It is an effect of the superabundance of the things of the Kingdom of God activating the things of earth. Human social life is thus superelevated in its own order by the supernatural ferment of the Gospel virtues. It is perfectly normal that a liturgical parish be also a parish in which Gospel charity vivifies the natural social community and the natural social activities, and develops in them the sense of social justice and of fraternal mutual help. To the work pursued by the liturgical renewal one already owes significant realizations accomplished in this spirit.

But it is quite otherwise with the pseudo-liturgical systematization. It confuses the orders, and instead of tending to elevate the human social element by the life of the spirit it tends to submit the spiritual life to the human social element. What we must reproach it for above all, it seems to us, is its pulling down to the plane of the human social what belongs of itself to the divine social. There is here a kind of insidious naturalism. It is then the nostalgia of common engagement, of the life of the team and the group, of the primacy of the social and the communal—so deeply felt by our age in the natural and temporal, terrestrial and human order—that one invokes and wishes to satisfy, and that one wishes to impose, in the very order of religious and spiritual life. It is a purely natural gregarious instinct that one seeks to satisfy in the name of the sacred liturgy, it is an *esse inter homines*—a "being among men"—that one demands in the name of the Mystical Body itself. Thence the suspicion towards private prayer, regarded as individualist and egocentric, and accepted only in the measure in which it prepares one for the better performing of public prayer and of the functions of worship. Thence the disregard of the person and of his singular relation with

God. The authentic human social realm recognizes in its own order the rights and the privileges of the person. But in the false perspective of which we are speaking one extends the human social claims outside of their own order, to impose them on a domain which is not their own and where they devour everything.

CHAPTER VI

Divine love is a love from Person to person

One ends up forgetting the personal character of the love that God demands of us, of each soul one by one—and not only of choirs of reciters. If our God loved only social masses praying and singing together (He loves them too), this would have been indicated by some commandment. But there is only the wholly personal commandment of love: *Thou* (and not you) shalt love thy God with *thy* whole heart, *thy* whole soul, *thy* whole mind. Now neither the heart nor the soul nor the mind are social things. They are individual or, better, personal; and the person is not an object that can be added up.

Consider the human assembly of a hundred thousand believers: they do not add up to form a mass that would be the sum of them all; they are persons each one of whom has the faith. It is not a single act of faith common to all, it is the act of faith proper to each one which is an offering pleasing to God.

If it is a question, it is true, of the supernatural society that is the Church, it is in virtue of a unique sap which is the life of their life, in virtue of the grace of Christ vivifying their most personal activities, that human persons are members of the Mystical Body. As an exterior sign of this communion, and of fraternal love among us, Jesus likes that we be several—even if only two or three —gathered together in His name. But persons are not added up there either, and it remains always that faith, hope and charity are strictly personal, like merit. As a member of a body whose common good is identical with the ultimate good itself of each person, each one is alone before God to love Him, to contemplate Him here below and to see Him in Heaven, as also to be judged by Him— each one according to his love.

This is why what counts in the contemplative life is always a wholly unique presence before God.

The love of God is always from Person to person, and our love for God is always from our heart to His heart which has loved us first,[11] in our very singularity—whether this love wells up in us at the recitation of liturgical texts, at the hearing of Gregorian chant or any other music worthy of accompanying the Divine Office, or at the solitary reading of the Bible, or in the wordless recollection and repose of prayer.

[11] It is thus that Henry Suso writes: "Once I saw spiritually that the heart of my heavenly Father was joined to mine in an ineffable manner. Yes, I felt the heart of God, divine Wisdom without form or image, who spoke to me in the innermost recesses of my heart, and in the swoon of my joy I exclaimed: 'O my sweet Beloved and my only Love, see how I embrace Thy divinity, heart to heart!'" (*Union of the Soul*, c. 3; cited by Arintero, *op. cit.*, vol. II, p. 276).

CHAPTER VII

The value of silence

Against the pseudo-liturgical state of mind it behooves one to defend the rights and the dignity of silence. In certain parishes into which this state of mind has penetrated, many of the faithful—so our friends in Europe write us—complain that in entering into church to meditate they are deafened by the noise. It is certain that the dialogue Mass,[12] as it is called, is a conquest of the liturgical renewal in its most authentic sense. It proves itself to be of incomparable assistance for the piety of a great many. Still it is necessary for the human voice to be humble in it, discreet and prayerful, not screeching. If on the other hand the solemn Mass is clearly the noblest and fullest form of the

---

[12] In his article in *Osservatore Romano* (October 2, 1958) on the subject of the Instruction of the Congregation of Rites mentioned below, Father Antonelli points out that the expression "dialogue Mass" is not too felicitous a one, for in what is called the dialogue Mass the faithful—in addition to the responses that they make to the priest, as in a dialogue—can recite with him several important parts like the *Gloria* and the *Credo*. (Cf. *Documentation Catholique*, November 9, 1958, p. 1438, note 23.)

celebration of the Holy Sacrifice, it would be folly however to claim to condemn low Masses for this reason—those low Masses of the dawn in which there descends upon the soul in silence, with an unequalled sweetness, the dew of the feasts and commemorations of each day.

As regards participation in the liturgical life of the Church, and although the expression "active participation" has in actual fact taken the sense of participation externally manifested, it is important to observe here that to *listen,* whether with the ear or with the heart, is from the philosophical point of view as "active" as to *speak.* No doubt it is preferable that the faithful manifest this participation outwardly by answering the priest and joining, at certain moments, their voices to his, even during low Masses, according as it is recommended in a recent Instruction of the Congregation of Rites.[13] If however these recommendations

[13] Instruction "De Musica sacra," *Acta Apostolicae Sedis,* September 19–22, 1958 (cf. *Documentation Catholique,* November 9, 1958).

When it treats of the "read Mass" (low Mass), this Instruction sanctions (art. 31) the Mass called (improperly) the dialogue Mass as the third and most perfect mode of participation of the faithful (itself implying four different degrees). However it also sanctions (art. 29) "the first way in which the faithful can participate in the read Mass" and in which "all, *on their own responsibility,* bring a participation *either interior, by giving a pious attention to the principal parts of the Mass,* or exterior, according to the different approved regional customs." (The words "on their own responsibility" are italicized by the Instruction itself; the other italics are ours.)

are not given as a categorical order imposed on each one, it is because, in the last analysis, those who prefer to nourish themselves on the prayer of the Church either by listening to the Gregorian chant at Office or at High Mass, or by piously reading the Missal to follow the action of the priest and to unite themselves with it, participate, to speak the truth, in the liturgical life of the Mystical Body in a manner as really active, although silent and not manifested (and in this less complete), as those who sing or who answer in a loud voice. And it remains in any case that *even when it speaks, humility listens.*[14]

Let us note finally with what care the Church maintains, even in the so-called dialogue Mass and in the solemn Mass, the part due to silence—to that very silence which is that of prayer *clauso ostio.* "From the Consecration to the *Pater,* silence is recommended." [15] "During the time of the Consecration, all singing, and, wherever it is the custom, even the music of the organ or of any other instrument must cease. After the Consecration, unless the *Benedictus* is still to be sung, a sacred silence is advised up to the *Pater noster.*" [16]

[14] Thomas Merton, *op. cit.,* p. 90.
[15] *Instruction* cited, art. 14, *c.*
[16] *Ibid.,* art. 27, *e* and *f.*

CHAPTER VIII

The liberty of souls

Against the pseudo-liturgical exaggerations it behooves one to defend the liberty of souls. This is what the Pope, Father and pastor of all, did, when he said in moving terms: "Many of the faithful are unable to use the 'Roman Missal' even though it is written in the vernacular; nor are all capable of understanding correctly the liturgical rites and formulas. So varied and diverse are men's talents and characters that it is impossible for all to be moved and attracted to the same extent by community prayers, hymns, and liturgical services. Moreover, the needs and inclinations of all are not the same, nor are they always constant in the same individual. Who then would say, on account of such a prejudice, that all these Christians cannot participate in the Mass nor share its fruits? On the contrary, they can adopt some other method which proves easier for certain people, for instance, they can lovingly meditate on the mysteries of Jesus Christ or perform other exercises of piety or recite prayers which, though they differ from the sacred rites, are still essentially in harmony with them." [17]

". . . It is perfectly clear to all," Pius XII writes again,[18] "that in the Church on earth, no less than in the Church in heaven, there are many mansions (John, XIV, 2). . . . It is the same Spirit Who breatheth where He will (John III, 8); and Who with differing gifts and in different ways enlightens and guides souls to sanctity. Let their freedom and the supernatural action of the Holy Spirit be so sacrosanct that no one presume to disturb or stifle them for any reason whatsoever."

Rome has always been vigilant in opposing any attempt to regiment souls. She knows that the spirit of the liturgy requires respect for the Gospel liberty proper to the New Law. On the contrary, in holding as valid one single form of piety, that in which each one acts in common with the others, and in demanding of all that by word and gesture they obey the liturgical forms with a military precision; in challenging or putting in question pri-

[17] *Mediator Dei,* p. 40.
[18] *Ibid.,* p. 61 (with respect to the exercises of Saint Ignatius and while recommending them especially).

vate devotions, nay even the adoration of the Blessed Sacrament outside of Mass, those who confuse liturgy and pseudo-liturgy impose on souls rigid frameworks and burden them with external obligations which are of the same type as the observances of the Old Law.

CHAPTER IX

In defense of the liturgy

Against pseudo-liturgy it behooves one to defend the liturgy. The latter, as we have observed, superabounds from the contemplation of the Church; it is in the inspired wisdom of the Church, and in its union of love with God, that is the supreme and most pure measure of the forms through which worship and public prayer are accomplished.

The liturgy can only suffer gravely from the spirit of system, or from a spirit of the arbitrary whether in novelty or in archaism, or from a fixation on the past which tends to disregard its homogeneous development inseparably bound to that of the life of the Church. These different kinds of excess have been denounced in the encyclical *Mediator Dei*.

CHAPTER X

In defense of solitude

It is clear that participation in the liturgical life of the Church is of itself eminently suited for preparing souls for supernatural recollection and contemplative union. The liturgy transmits to us in its signs an expression of the charity and contemplation of the Church itself. Nothing is richer in meaning than its rites and its great poetry, its prayers, its lessons, its hymns and its psalms. In a continuous and exultant reiteration it enlightens our minds with the light of the Old and the New Testaments, and it puts on our lips the words uttered by the most venerable contemplatives, prayers of David, messages of the Prophets, teachings of the Fathers. And to the one who follows it each day with all the attention of his heart, it brings a continuous spiritual stimulation, and often responses and inspirations singularly appropriate to his personal life; it awakens him to the aspirations of his own soul at the same time as to the mysteries of the cycle of Time and of the cycle of the Saints.

If participation in the liturgical life (on condition that it be animated by fervor, and not deadened by routine) thus constitutes a particularly excellent way to prepare the soul for contemplation, it is however far from taking the place of ascetical preparations and from rendering them superfluous. It is neither the only way nor the indispensable way towards contemplation. Still less would it be, as the pseudo-liturgical excesses would have it, necessarily required for the perfection of the spiritual life independently of all ordination to contemplation, and as a sort of absolute sufficient unto itself.

Why should the possibility of attaining to a perfectly pure spiritual life be reserved to a privileged elite devoted to the liturgical service? There is the multitude of others, whom the obligations of life and the exigencies of work impede. There are those charged with family responsibilities, the itinerants, the sick, the illiterate, there are the solitaries. . . .

Against pseudo-liturgy it behooves one to defend solitude and the solitary life. The soul breathes in solitude, a certain amount of solitude is indispensable for the life of the spirit: "The ears with which one hears the message of the Gospel are hidden in man's heart, and these ears do not hear anything unless they are favored with a certain interior solitude and silence. . . . We listen to the Father best in solitude." [19] "The more our soul finds itself alone and separated," wrote Saint Ignatius of Loyola,[20] "the more it renders itself capable of approaching its Creator and Lord and of attaining Him."

In solitude she lived
And in solitude now has built her nest,
And in solitude her dear one alone guides her . . .[21]

As to the solitary life, it is the state of life at once the most difficult and the most elevated.[22] Eternally snow-clad summit from which descend the life-giving rivers, this state of life will never be missing from the Church. With the Carthusians it is certainly not exclusive of the liturgical service and of the most beautiful chants, but the Office chanted in common is of less importance than the Solitary Dialogue with God. With the hermits

[19] Thomas Merton, *op. cit.,* pp. 13, 106.
[20] In his Twentieth Note.
[21] Saint John of the Cross, *Spiritual Canticle* (translation of E. Allison Peers).
[22] *Sum. theol.,* II–II, 188, 8.

there is no longer anything but the Solitary Dialogue with God. There is no longer any public prayer; there is no longer any liturgical service (except, for the priests, the read Mass and the private recitation of the Office). It is in pure solitude that a Father de Foucauld attained a sublime contemplation and an heroic perfection.

Saint Benedict Labre was not a hermit, but a beggar, or rather a seeker of God on the roads of the earth, completely cut off from the world by total poverty, vermin and beggary; and in this respect he was more retired from men and more alone than even a hermit.

Solitude of Saint Benedict Labre! Solitude is his vocation—whether he be lost in the outlying wilderness or amidst the people of Rome. Contemplation must be his whole life in the time before the eternal Beatitude.

He has to leave the convent in which he thought he was to pass his life; he has only to go along the roads and pray . . . often in anguish and darkness.

He has no other desire than the solitary life in the midst of infinite privations—in the glowing presence of God, of Him who requires him in his entirety.

Such is then his life. He goes along the roads with God.

He doesn't need anything of this world. Total poverty is for him a gift from Heaven—poverty, solitude; and silence. His prayer is prayer of humility and of love, of charity and of light, of fire and of ecstasy. He sings in the forests.

Over the long ways of France and Italy, walking barefooted, he reaches Rome. Doubtless it was a sacred desire of his. He has come to the home of Saint Peter and Saint Paul, and to the tomb of innumerable martyrs.

He frequents a small and very humble church, Santa Maria dei Monti, where his body and the tomb statue of him are today.

He assisted at Mass there, received Holy Communion, had his habitual ecstasies and his raptures there. The poor people of the district venerated this other poor one, this one who needed only the love of God, this strange being who was ignorant of the attractions of terrestrial forces, and whom God drew to Himself.

In Rome at Santa Maria dei Monti, at the Coliseum, in the streets where the children made fun of him, he lived his divine life. Alone and ever in the presence of God, of His love, of His light.